Where We Live

Canada

Donna Bailey

STECK-VAUGHN
LIBRARY
A Division of Steck-Vaughn Company

Hello! My name is Susan.

I live in the country near

Jasper National Park in Alberta, Canada.

Jasper National Park is a very beautiful
part of Canada with many rivers,
mountains, and lakes.

In the winter, heavy snows fall
in the mountains.
The road from Jasper has to be
cleared after a heavy snow.

Canadian winters can be very cold.
In the winter, we usually get enough snow
to build giant snowpeople in our yard.

One of our winter chores is to make sure
we have enough logs to feed the fire
to keep us warm.
We all help Dad gather the wood.

Dad also has to clear the driveway
so that he can get the car out.
He uses a machine that cuts into
the snow and blows it away.

We get up early every morning.
After breakfast I help clear the dishes and
then it is time to get ready for school.

We wrap up warmly and my brother John and
I walk down to the main road.
We meet our friend and wait for
the school bus to pick us up.

I have lots of friends at school.
Our school is built for cold and hot weather.
In winter central heating keeps
our classroom warm.
In summer air-conditioning keeps
our classroom cool.

Mom often meets me after school and
we go shopping at the market
on the way home.

On the weekend we usually go skiing.
I love to go really fast downhill
on my short skis.
Dad prefers cross-country skiing because
he can go for miles through the woods.

During the summer we usually go
on vacation.
We travel in a small sea plane that
can land on water.

We visit our friends who have a summer home
on the shores of Lake Ontario.
We have fun swimming, boating, and fishing
in the lake.

We go fishing in our friends' canoe.
John enjoys fishing, but
I think it's more fun
to help Dad paddle the canoe.

We usually catch several fish.

When we get home, Dad cleans the fish.

We like to cook it on
the barbecue and eat outdoors.

We also go horseback riding
with our friends.
Sometimes we take our camping gear and
camp overnight in the wilderness.

Many young people in Alberta learn
to ride horses.
Good riders enjoy going on
trail rides in the wilderness.
The best riders take part in
the Calgary Stampede.

Calgary is an important town in
southern Alberta.
In the countryside near Calgary
people raise cattle and horses
on large ranches.

Every year in early July, the cowhands
round up the cattle.
They choose the best animals to take
to the international stock show that
is held during the Calgary Stampede.

Every morning, the stampede starts
with a special breakfast.
Men and women cook pancakes
outside their chuckwagon and serve breakfast
to visitors.

Everyone has fun during the ten days
of the Stampede in Calgary.
Musicians of all ages play the fiddle while
people sing and dance in the streets.

During the Stampede, people dress up
in rodeo clothes.
Most people wear a western hat even if
they don't have western-style boots.

On the first day of the Stampede,
the Native Americans wear
their traditional costumes.

In Stampede Park, visitors can see
a Native American camp and
learn how a tepee is built.

The most exciting part of the Stampede
is the rodeo that is held every afternoon.
The world's top riders compete against
each other in the rodeo.

Bull riding is one of the most
dangerous rodeo events.
Clowns encourage the bull to
buck harder as it tries to
throw the rider off its back.

The rider holds on to the bull with one hand and tries to stay on the animal for eight seconds. The rider's free hand must not touch the bull or the tack or the rider is disqualified.

In another competition, riders try to stay on
the back of a bucking bronco.
A bronco is a wild horse that
has never been tamed.
The rider mounts the bronco in its pen.
Then the bronco is let loose into the ring.

Every evening there is a chuckwagon race.
Each driver has four horses hitched to
a chuckwagon.
Only four wagons and their outriders
take part in each race.

Chuckwagon racing takes skill and daring.
When they hear the signal, the teams
pull away from the starting line and
race for the finish.

Later as the sun goes down, the arena
is cleared for the evening show.
The Royal Canadian Mounted Police
show their riding skill.
Dancers and singers from all over the world
entertain the crowds.

Index

Editorial Consultant: Donna Bailey
Executive Editor: Elizabeth Strauss
Project Editor: Becky Ward

Picture research by Jennifer Garratt
Designed by Richard Garratt Design

Photographs
Cover: Hutchison (Nancy Durrell McKenna)
Alberta Government Photos: 21, 22, 24, 25, 28, 29, 30
Robert Estall: 19
Hutchison: title page, 2, 5, 6, 7, 8, 9, 10, 11, 12, 13, 15, 16, 18 (Nancy Durrell McKenna),
14 (John Downman)
Spectrum Colour Library: 26, 27, 31
Zefa: 3, 4, 20, 23, 32
Peter Greenland: 17

Library of Congress Cataloging-in-Publication Data: Bailey, Donna. Canada/written by Donna Bailey.
p.   cm.—(Where we live) Includes index. SUMMARY: A young girl describes her home and family and the
various features of their life in Alberta, Canada. ISBN 0-8114-2568-1 1. Alberta—Social life and customs—
Juvenile literature. 2. Outdoor life—Alberta—Juvenile literature. [1. Alberta—Social life and customs.
2. Canada—Social life and customs.] I. Title. F1071.B35   1991   971.23′32—dc20   91-21292   CIP   AC

ISBN 0-8114-2568-1
Copyright 1992 Steck-Vaughn Company
Original copyright Heinemann Children's Reference 1991

1 2 3 4 5 6 7 8 9 0 LB 97 96 95 94 93 92